Explore new ideas!

Animal Discoveries

Read exciting literature, science and social studies texts!

Become an expert writer!

Build vocabulary and knowledge to unlock the Wonders of reading!

Use your student login to explore your interactive Reading/Writing Workshop, practice close reading, and more.

Go Digital! www.connected.mcgraw-hill.com

(tl) Alistair Berg/Digital Vision/Getty Images; (rb) Wave/Photolibrary; (rt) Mike Litwin; (b) Nathan Love

Cover and Title Pages: Nathan Love

www.mheonline.com/readingwonders

Send all inquiries to:
McGraw-Hill Education
Two Penn Plaza
New York, NY 10121

ISBN: 978-0-07-898075-6
MHID: 0-07-898075-5

Printed in the United States of America.

1 2 3 4 5 6 7 8 9 LWI 22 21 20 19 18 17   A

Wonders

An English Language Arts Program

Program Authors

Diane August

Donald R. Bear

Janice A. Dole

Jana Echevarria

Douglas Fisher

David Francis

Vicki Gibson

Jan Hasbrouck

Margaret Kilgo

Jay McTighe

Scott G. Paris

Timothy Shanahan

Josefina V. Tinajero

Mc
Graw
Hill
Education

Unlock the
Wonders
of
Reading

With your *Reading/Writing Workshop* you will:

- Closely read and reread literature and informational text

- Discuss what you have read with your peers

- Become a better writer and researcher

- Look for text evidence as you respond to complex text

Get Ready to Become:

- Lifelong Learners
- Critical Thinkers
- Part of the Community of Learning

READ and REREAD

Exciting Literature

Fables, folktales, and fantasies will take you to new worlds. Through stories and poems discover new wonders. It's all waiting for you!

Informational Texts

Read about amazing people and brave heroes. Informational text will open up the worlds of Science and Social Studies.

ACT
Access Complex Text

As you read, take notes on what you don't understand. Look at the questions below. They will help you move in the right direction.

VOCABULARY

What can I do if I come across a word I don't know? I can look for context clues or look up the word in a dictionary.

MAKE CONNECTIONS

Can I connect ideas in the text to help me understand what the author wants to explain or describe?

ILLUSTRATIONS AND TEXT FEATURES

Does the selection have features, such as an illustration, a map, or a diagram, that can help me to understand the text?

TEXT STRUCTURE

How is the text organized? Can I find a cause or an effect? Are there steps that tell me how to do something? Knowing the text structure helps me understand what I am reading.

COLLABORATE What do you do when you don't understand something you read?

L👀k for Text Evidence

When you answer a question about your reading, you often have to look for evidence in the text to support or even find the answer. Here are some tips to help you find what you are looking for.

Maria thinks about her father's words. Pai is right. She and the other children have worked hard for a year. They practiced their dance steps over and over. They even made their own bright colorful costumes.

Stated
Here I can locate information that tells me that Maria put a lot of effort into this celebration.

One week passes. Lots of people line the streets. The children in Maria's group are wearing their sparkling costumes. They know each dance step. They dance to the beat.

Unstated
This text evidence allows me to make the inference that Maria's hard work paid off in the end.

Text Evidence

Sometimes you will find the answers right there in the text. Sometimes you need to look for clues in different parts of text and put the answer in your own words.

It's Stated—Right There!

Some questions ask you to locate details, such as *Who made Maria's costume?* The answers are usually found in a sentence you can point to.

You need to combine clues to answer other questions such as *Why did Maria need to go to practice?* Look in more than one place in the text for the answer.

It's Not Stated—But Here's My Evidence!

Sometimes the answers are not stated in the text. Think of a question like *How did Maria feel when she was marching in the parade?* To answer it, you look for important details or clues. Then you put the clues in your own words to answer the question.

COLLABORATE

Point to the right there evidence that tells you who made Maria's costume.

Be an Expert Writer

Remember that good writing presents clear ideas. It is well organized and contains evidence and details from reliable sources. See how Alex answered a question about a text he read.

Alex's Model

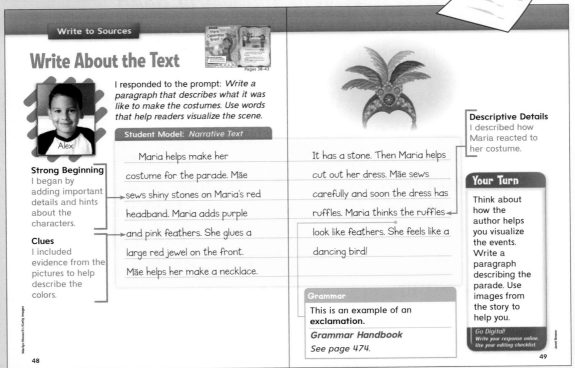

Write to Sources

Write About the Text

Pages 38–43

I responded to the prompt: *Write a paragraph that describes what it was like to make the costumes. Use words that help readers visualize the scene.*

Alex

Student Model: *Narrative Text*

Maria helps make her costume for the parade. Mãe sews shiny stones on Maria's red headband. Maria adds purple and pink feathers. She glues a large red jewel on the front. Mãe helps her make a necklace.

It has a stone. Then Maria helps cut out her dress. Mãe sews carefully and soon the dress has ruffles. Maria thinks the ruffles look like feathers. She feels like a dancing bird!

Strong Beginning
I began by adding important details and hints about the characters.

Clues
I included evidence from the pictures to help describe the colors.

Descriptive Details
I described how Maria reacted to her costume.

Your Turn

Think about how the author helps you visualize the events. Write a paragraph describing the parade. Use images from the story to help you.

Go Digital!
Write your response online. Use your editing checklist.

Grammar
This is an example of an **exclamation**.
Grammar Handbook
See page 474.

48

49

Write About the Text

When you write about something you have read closely, introduce your topic clearly. Use details from the text. When you do research, make sure you use reliable sources. Use the checklist below.

Opinions Did I support opinions with facts and evidence? Did I use linking words such as *because* to connect my ideas? Did I write a strong conclusion?

Informative Texts Did I develop the topic with facts from the text? Did I write a conclusion that connected all my information?

Narrative Texts When you write a narrative, you use your imagination to develop real or made-up events. The checklist below will help you write memorable stories.

- **Sequence** Did I use words that help tell the sequence of events?

- **Descriptive Details** Did I include details to describe actions in the narrative?

What is your favorite thing to write about? Tell a partner why.

Unit 2 Animal Discoveries

The Big Idea

How do animals play a part
in the world around us?. **96**

Go Digital! Find all lessons online at www.connected.mcgraw-hill.com.

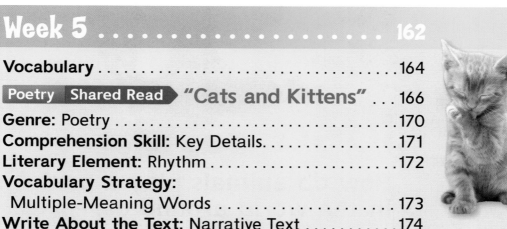

Animal Discoveries

The
Big Idea

How do animals play a part in the world around us?

Animals Are Amazing

Kittens mew and dogs play catch,
Ducks and hens lay eggs to hatch.
    Animals are amazing!

Bees make honey, lambs give wool,
Horses gallop, oxen pull.

Big game lions prowl and roar,
Turtles crawl and eagles soar.

Animals at work and play,
All around me, night and day.
    Animals are amazing!

by Winifred Califano

Animal Survival

Meerkats live in hot, dry places. Here are some ways they adapt to the heat.

► They live in underground burrows.

► They have thin fur.

► They search for food in the early morning hours when it is cool.

Talk About It

Talk with a partner about how animals survive in hot climates. Write your ideas on the web.

Vocabulary

Use the picture and sentence to learn each word.

adapt

The polar bear's thick fur coat helps it **adapt** to the icy water.

How do you adapt to cold weather?

climate

Tom lives in a hot and sunny **climate**.

What is the climate like where you live?

eager

Mindy is **eager** to see her grandmother.

What is something that you are eager to do?

freedom

Deer have the **freedom** to move about the open land.

What animals are free to roam about the forest?

fresh

The baker made **fresh** bread every day.

What word means the opposite of *fresh*?

sense

I felt a **sense** of pride when I won the race.

When do you feel a sense of pride?

shadows

We made animal **shadows** on the wall.

What shadows can you make?

silence

The baby needed **silence** to fall asleep.

What word means the same as silence?

COLLABORATE

Your Turn

Pick three words. Write three questions for your partner to answer.

Go Digital! *Use the online visual glossary*

A Visit to the Desert

Inquiry Question

What can we learn from animals in stories?

Greg Newbold

102

Tim was looking forward to this vacation. Then his parents told him the family would be visiting Grandma in Nevada. Tim was unhappy. He wanted to be with his friends this summer.

"Grandma is **eager** to see you," Mom said. "She can't wait to take you on a desert hike."

The next morning Grandma met them at the airport. Then they drove to the desert. As they hiked, Grandma explained that animals enjoy the open desert space. It gives them the **freedom** to move from place to place. Tim learned that the animals find ways to **adapt** to the hot desert weather. He wondered if he could get used to the desert **climate**.

Greg Newbold

"Wow," Tim said, "look at that! The turtle carries its home on its back!"

Grandma smiled at Tim's excitement. "Actually," she said, "that is a desert tortoise. It looks for the shade made by the **shadows** of rocks. That's how it cools off. He burrows underground to get away from the heat." The tortoise disappeared into its burrow. Tim leaned over the hole. He could not hear a sound.

"I'll bet it likes the **silence** of its burrow," Tim whispered.

"I think it likes its **sense** of safety too," Grandma added.

"That's the same feeling I get at home," Tim sighed. Just then a large rabbit hopped by. Grandma explained that the jack rabbit's large ears help it stay cool.

"These animals are so unlike the animals at home!" Tim said. He had forgotten about the desert heat.

"Some animals stay cool by sleeping during the day. Then they hunt at night," said Grandma. A Great Horned Owl hooted above them. Grandma said, "It will soon be time for the owl to hunt."

"Which means it's time for us to head back," Dad added.

"Aw, this vacation is going by too fast," Tim said. They asked Tim about the heat. "What heat?" Tim asked. "I feel as **fresh** and cool as a new flower. I've adapted!" Everyone laughed.

Make Connections

How does the desert tortoise survive in the heat?

Think of another animal you know. How does it survive in its climate?

TEXT TO SELF

Make Predictions

Use what you already know and what you read in the story to help you predict, or guess, what might happen next.

 Find Text Evidence

After reading page 104 of "A Visit to the Desert," I predicted that Tim would enjoy his visit to the desert. I kept reading to confirm my prediction.

> **page 105**
>
> "Wow," Tim said, "look at that! The turtle carries its home on its back!"
>
> Grandma smiled at Tim's excitement. "Actually," she said, "that is a desert tortoise. It looks for the shade made by the **shadows** of rocks. That's how it cools off. He burrows underground to get away from the heat." The tortoise disappeared into its burrow. Tim leaned over the hole. He could not hear a sound.

On page 105, I read that Tim was excited to learn about different desert animals. I confirmed my prediction.

Your Turn

COLLABORATE

Reread page 105. What did you predict would happen next? Look for clues in the text to decide if your prediction was correct.

Greg Newbold

Plot

The plot is the events that happen in the beginning, middle and end of the story.

 Find Text Evidence

When I read "A Visit to the Desert," I think about the plot, or what happens in the story.

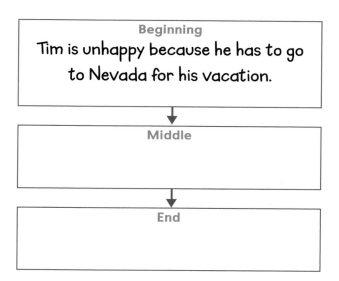

Beginning
Tim is unhappy because he has to go to Nevada for his vacation.

↓

Middle

↓

End

Your Turn

COLLABORATE

Continue reading the story. Finish writing the plot in the graphic organizer.

Go Digital!
Use the interactive graphic organizer

Realistic Fiction

The story "A Visit to the Desert" is realistic fiction. **Realistic fiction**:
- is a story that could happen in real life.
- has characters that could be real people.

Find Text Evidence

I can tell from the text that "A Visit to the Desert" is realistic fiction. Tim acts like a real person. He wonders if he can get used to the heat.

page 104

The next morning Grandma met them at the airport. Then they drove to the desert. As they hiked, Grandma explained that animals enjoy the open desert space. It gives them the **freedom** to move from place to place. Tim learned that the animals find ways to **adapt** to the hot desert weather. He wondered if he could get used to the desert **climate**.

104

Use Illustrations

The illustrations show me that Tim and his family are visiting a desert. I know that could happen in real life.

Your Turn

Give two examples of how you know this story is realistic fiction.

Greg Newbold

Prefixes

A prefix is a word part at the beginning of a word. You can separate a prefix, such as *un-* or *dis-,* from the root word.

Find Text Evidence

I'm not sure what the word unhappy *means. I know that* happy *means to feel good about something. The prefix* un- *means not. I think the word means* not happy.

Tim was unhappy.

Your Turn

Use prefixes to figure out the meanings of the following words in "A Visit to the Desert."

unlike, page 106

disappeared, *page 105*

Greg Newbold

Write About the Text

Pages 102–107

Olivia

I responded to the prompt: *Add an event to the story. Have Grandma explain why she wanted Tim to come with her to the desert.*

Student Model: *Narrative Text*

Event
I added where Grandma took Tim.

Descriptive Details
I described several reasons to help explain Grandma's actions.

Before heading home, Tim and Grandma went on an evening hike. Grandma talked about how much she liked living here. She pointed out the different animals that came out in the evening. She spoke about how bright the stars were at night.

"I wanted to share all of this with you," Grandma told Tim.

"I wanted you to hike the trails I found. I wanted you to see the animals that live here. I wanted you to see the beauty of the environment. Now, when we talk, you can picture the desert in your mind."

Details

I included evidence to show Grandma's thoughts and feelings about living in the desert.

Grammar

This is an example of a **noun**. A desert is a place.

Grammar Handbook

See page 477.

Your Turn

Pretend you are Tim. Explain to your parents how your feelings changed during the trip.

Go Digital!
Write your response online.
Use your editing checklist.

Greg Newbold

What can animals in stories teach us?

 Go Digital!

Mircea Catusanu

114

Animal Lessons

Do you know the story of the Tortoise and the Hare? The Hare is ahead in a race with a slow Tortoise so he decides to take a nap. Then Tortoise ends up winning the race!

▶ Animals in stories teach us lessons.

▶ Animals in stories help us learn about each other.

Talk About It

Talk with a partner about the lessons we learn from animals in stories. Write the lessons on the word web.

Vocabulary

Use the picture and sentence to learn each word.

believe I **believe** it is going to rain today.

What is something you believe will happen today?

delicious We ate the **delicious** pizza.

Describe something that tastes delicious.

feast Our family sat at the dinner table and started to **feast**.

When might you feast?

fond Rob is very **fond** of his puppy.

What is something that you are fond of?

(t)Fancy/Alamy; (tc)BananaStock/PunchStock; (bc)JGI/Blend Images/Getty Images; (b)Ryan McVay/Photolibrary

lessons

I learned a lot from the teacher's **lessons**.

What lessons do you learn at school?

remarkable

I saw a **remarkable** rainbow in the sky.

Describe something that is remarkable.

snatch

My dog can **snatch** a flying disc out of the air.

Show how you would snatch something off your desk.

stories

Our dad reads us **stories** before bedtime.

What are some stories you like?

COLLABORATE

Your Turn

Pick three words. Write three questions for your partner to answer.

Go Digital! *Use the online visual glossary*

The Boy Who Cried Wolf

Inquiry Question

What can we learn from animals in stories?

Peter Francis

118

Long ago a shepherd boy sat on a hilltop watching the village sheep. He was not **fond** of his job. He didn't like it one bit. He would have liked something wonderful to happen, but nothing **remarkable** ever did.

The shepherd boy watched the clouds move softly by to stay busy. He saw horses, dogs, and dragons in the sky. He made up **stories** with these things as characters.

119

Then one day he had a better idea! He took a deep breath and cried out, "Wolf! Wolf! The wolf is chasing the sheep!"

The villagers ran up the hill to help the boy. When they got there, they saw no harmful wolf. The boy laughed. "Shepherd boy! Don't cry 'wolf!' unless there really is a wolf!" said the villagers. They went back down the hill.

Peter Francis

That afternoon the boy again cried out, "Wolf! Wolf! The wolf is chasing the sheep!"

The villagers ran to help the boy again. They saw no wolf. The villagers were angry. "Don't cry 'wolf!' when there is NO WOLF!" they said. The shepherd boy just smiled. The villagers went quickly down the hill again.

That afternoon the boy saw a REAL wolf. He did not want the wolf to grab any of the sheep! The boy thought the wolf would **snatch** one of them for a **delicious**, tasty meal. A sheep would be a big **feast** for a wolf. He quickly jumped to his feet and cried, "WOLF! WOLF!" The villagers thought he was tricking them again, so they did not come.

That night the shepherd boy did not return with their sheep. The villagers found the boy weeping real tears. "There really was a wolf here!" he said. "The flock ran away! When I cried out, 'Wolf! Wolf!' no one came. Why didn't you come?"

Peter Francis

122

A kind man talked to the boy as they walked slowly back to the village. "In the morning, we'll help you look for the sheep," he said. "You have just learned one of life's important **lessons**. This is something you need to know. Nobody **believes** a person who tells lies. It is always better to tell the truth!"

Make Connections

What did you learn after reading this animal story?

Tell how you are similar or different from the shepherd boy. TEXT TO SELF

Make Predictions

Use what you read in the story to help you predict, or guess, what might happen next.

 Find Text Evidence

On page 120 of "The Boy Who Cried Wolf," I predicted that the boy will upset the villagers.

page 121

That afternoon the boy again cried out, "Wolf! Wolf! The wolf is chasing the sheep!"

The villagers ran to help the boy again. They saw no wolf. The villagers were angry. "Don't cry 'wolf!' when there is NO WOLF!" they said. The shepherd boy just smiled. The villagers went quickly down the hill again.

On page 121, I read that the villagers were angry with the boy. I confirmed my prediction.

Your Turn

COLLABORATE

When the boy saw the wolf, what did you predict would happen? Point to the place in the text that confirmed your prediction.

Peter Francis

Problem and Solution

The plot is often about the problem in the story. The solution is how the characters solve the problem by the end of the story.

 Find Text Evidence

In the beginning of "The Boy Who Cried Wolf," I read about the boy's problem of being bored.

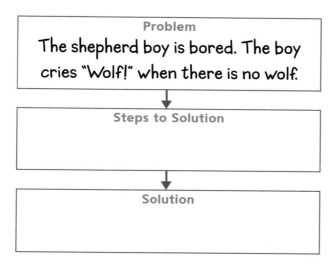

Problem

The shepherd boy is bored. The boy cries "Wolf!" when there is no wolf.

↓

Steps to Solution

↓

Solution

Your Turn

Finish rereading the story. Think about how the problem got solved. Fill in the boxes on the graphic organizer.

Go Digital!
Use the interactive graphic organizer

Fable

"The Boy Who Cried Wolf" is a fable. A **fable**:
- is a made-up story that teaches a lesson.
- has a beginning, middle and end.

Find Text Evidence

I can use what I read to tell that "The Boy Who Cried Wolf" is a fable. It is a made-up story that has a beginning, middle, and end.

page 119

Long ago a shepherd boy sat on a hilltop watching the village sheep. He was not **fond** of his job. He didn't like it one bit. He would have liked something wonderful to happen, but nothing **remarkable** ever did.

The shepherd boy watched the clouds move softly by to stay busy. He saw horses, dogs, and dragons in the sky. He made up **stories** with these things as characters.

119

Story Structure

In the **beginning** of the fable, the shepherd boy is bored and plays a trick on the villagers. In the **middle** of the story, the villagers try to teach the boy a lesson.

Your Turn

COLLABORATE

Tell how the boy learns a lesson at the **end** of the story.

Suffixes

A suffix is a word part or syllable added to the end of a word. You can separate the root word from a suffix, such as *-ful* or *-ly*, to figure out what the word means.

 Find Text Evidence

I'm not sure what the word harmful *means. The root word is* harm, *which means "to hurt." The suffix is* -ful *which means "full of." I think the word* harmful *means "full of hurt."*

When they got there, they saw no harmful wolf.

Your Turn

Use suffixes to figure out the meanings of these words in "The Boy Who Cried Wolf."
wonderful, *page 119*
softly, *page 119*

Peter Francis

Pages 118–123

Write About the Text

Mia

I responded to the prompt: *Add an event to the end of the story. Have the shepherd apologize to the villagers.*

Student Model: *Narrative Text*

Reasons

I explained what the shepherd boy said to make the beginning strong.

In the morning, the shepherd boy talked to the villagers. He said, "I'm sorry that I lied about the wolf. I'm sorry that your sheep ran away. I have learned a lesson. From now on, I will always tell the truth. I'll try to keep the sheep safe."

Grammar

The word *villagers* is a **plural noun**.

Grammar Handbook

See page 479.

First, the villagers forgave the shepherd boy. Then, they helped the boy find the sheep. The shepherd boy learned to like his job and became the best shepherd in the land.

Organizaton

I used time words to organize my story.

Supporting Details

I used ideas, to show why the villagers helped the boy find the sheep.

Your Turn

Add an event to the story. Tell what the boy does the next day instead of crying wolf.

Go Digital!
Write your response online.
Use your editing checklist.

Peter Francis

What are features of different animal habitats?

Go Digital!

Animal Homes

Hi! I'm an owl. I live in a special place in nature. I live in a forest habitat. Here's why:

► My feathers are the same colors as the trees. This helps me hide from predators.

► I can live inside this hole. My babies will be safe.

Talk About It

Talk with a partner about why animals live in forest habitats. Write your ideas on the web.

Vocabulary

Use the picture and sentence to learn each word.

buried The car was **buried** in the deep snow.

What buried things have you found?

escape The cat could **escape** through a hole in the fence.

What are other ways an animal could escape from a backyard?

habitat Prairie dogs live in a desert **habitat**.

What animals live in a forest habitat?

journey Maya and her family went on a **journey** in the woods.

What is another word for journey?

nature We walk in the woods because we like to be in **nature**.

What do you like about nature?

peeks While hiding, Kate **peeks** out from behind the tree.

Show how a person peeks out from behind something.

restless The child became **restless** during the long car ride.

When have you felt restless?

spies Carlos **spies** an eagle in the sky.

What is a synonym for spies?

Your Turn

COLLABORATE

Pick three words. Write three questions for your partner to answer.

Go Digital! *Use the online visual glossary*

A Prairie Guard Dog

Jeff Foott/Getty Images

Inquiry Question

How do animals survive?

I am on a **journey**. My trip is to a prairie. It is in the outdoor world called **nature**. Many animals live in a prairie **habitat**. This place has what prairie dogs need to survive. A prairie has a lot of grasses but few trees. Without places to hide, a prairie can be dangerous for some animals.

Good Morning!

It is early in the morning. First, I see a prairie dog. I name him Pete. He **peeks** his head out of his **burrow** underground. He looks around. Then Pete calls loudly to his family, "Yip!" He lets them know it is safe to come out. Soon four prairie dogs come out.

Prairie dogs build underground burrows to keep themselves safe from predators.

Pete is the guard and he is **restless**. He cannot rest because he is always looking around for danger. This allows the other prairie dogs to safely munch on grasses and seeds. They can also groom each other or work on their burrow.

Yap! Yap!

Prairie dogs can make 11 different sounds to communicate with each other.

A Scare

Oh no! Pete **spies** a large badger! When he sees it, he gives a loud bark, "Yap! Yap!" His family recognizes the warning. Some hide in tall grasses, and some jump into the burrow. The badger runs at Pete, but the watchful guard is able to **escape** into the burrow. I am glad he is able to get away from danger.

After a few minutes, Pete peeks his head out again and he is back on the job.

Badgers live on prairies and hunt prairie dogs.

Break Time

The sun gets higher, and it is hot now. The prairie dogs slip into their deep burrow where it is cooler. Even Pete goes in. **Tunnels**, like hallways, lead to different areas. There is a sleeping room. There is a room used like a bathroom. The prairie dogs cover up roots and seeds in one room. Later, they eat the **buried** food there.

Second Shift

I keep watching the burrow. Finally, the sun begins to set and a different prairie dog peeks its head out. I name him Gary. Pete must be off duty. "Yip," Gary calls. The other prairie dogs come back out.

The prairie dogs eat and play until the moon is high in the sky. Then they go to sleep in their burrows. I wonder if Pete will be back on duty. I will see in the morning.

Prairie Dog Facts	
Size	12 to 15 inches tall
Weight	2 to 4 pounds
Habitat	short and medium grass desert prairies
Food	roots, seeds, leaves of plants, grasses
Shelter	underground burrows with many rooms
Predators	coyotes, bobcats, badgers, foxes, weasels

Make Connections

What are two features of a prairie dog's habitat?

What animal did the prairie dog remind you of?

TEXT TO SELF

(bkgd) Bob Stefko/Getty Images

139

Make Predictions

Use what you already know and what you read in the selection to help you predict what you will learn about. As you read, you can confirm or revise your predictions.

 Find Text Evidence

As I read page 137 of "A Prairie Guard Dog," I predicted that the badger will chase the prairie dog. I read on to see if my prediction was correct.

page 137

A Scare

Oh no! Pete **spies** a large badger! When he sees it, he gives a loud bark, "Yap! Yap!" His family recognizes the warning. Some hide in tall grasses, and some jump into the burrow. The badger runs at Pete, but the watchful guard is able to **escape** into the burrow. I am glad he is able to get away from danger.

On page 137, I read that the badger ran at Pete. My prediction was correct.

COLLABORATE

Your Turn

Reread page 138. What did you predict would happen next? Look for text clues to decide if your prediction was correct.

Main Topic and Key Details

The main topic is what the selection is about. Key details give information about the main topic.

 Find Text Evidence

As I read "A Prairie Guard Dog," I learn a lot about prairie dogs. This must be the main topic. On page 135, I learn a key detail about prairie dogs.

Main Topic		
Prairie Dogs		
Key Detail	**Key Detail**	**Key Detail**
A prairie dog acts as a guard.		

COLLABORATE

Your Turn

Continue rereading the story. Fill in key details about the main topic on the graphic organizer.

Go Digital!
Use the interactive graphic organizer

Narrative Nonfiction

"A Prairie Guard Dog" is narrative nonfiction.
A **Narrative Nonfiction**:
- tells about living things, people, or events.
- is told by a narrator and follows a sequence.

Find Text Evidence

I can use what I read to tell that "A Prairie Guard Dog" is a narrative nonfiction. A narrator tells the story about what real prairie dogs do.

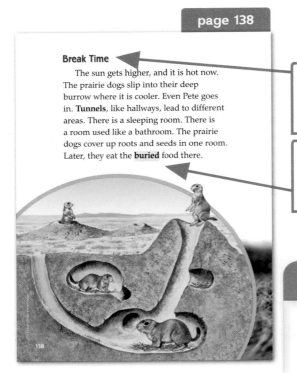

page 138

Break Time

The sun gets higher, and it is hot now. The prairie dogs slip into their deep burrow where it is cooler. Even Pete goes in. **Tunnels**, like hallways, lead to different areas. There is a sleeping room. There is a room used like a bathroom. The prairie dogs cover up roots and seeds in one room. Later, they eat the **buried** food there.

138

Text Features

Headings Headings tell what a section of text is mostly about.

Bold Print These words are important to understanding the text.

Your Turn
COLLABORATE

Identify text features on a different page. Tell what information you learned from these features.

Suffixes

A suffix is a word part or syllable added to the end of a word. You can separate the root word from a suffix, such as *-ful* or *-ly*, to figure out what the word means.

 Find Text Evidence

I'm not sure what the word loudly *means. The root word is* loud, *which means "full of noise." The suffix is* -ly *which means "in a certain way." I think the word* loudly *means "in a noisy way."*

Then, Pete calls loudly to his family, "Yip!"

Your Turn

 COLLABORATE

Use suffixes to figure out the meanings of these words in "A Prairie Guard Dog."
safely, *page 136*
watchful, *page 137*
finally, *page 139*

Corbis Flirt/Alamy

Write About the Text

Pages 134–139

I answered the question: *How did the author organize the text from the beginning to the end? Tell why.*

Stella

Student Model: *Informative Text*

The author organizes the text from morning to night. The author did this to help me learn how prairie dogs live. Learning about Pete helps me learn about guarding something.

The author begins by telling what Pete does in the morning.

Grammar

The word *morning* is a **common noun**.

Grammar Handbook

See pages 477–478.

Sequence

I used the time of day to logically organize the text.

Then the author tells me what Pete does in the afternoon. The text ends at night when the moon is high in the sky and the prairie dogs sleep in their burrows.

Supporting Details
I included facts from the selection about the moon to show the different time of day.

Strong Conclusion
My last sentence sums up the ideas in my answer.

Your Turn

How does the use of text features help tell the story? Include text evidence to support your answer.

Go Digital!
Write your response online.
Use your editing checklist.

Animal
Babies and Parents

This baby penguin and his mother look different but they are the same in many ways.

► They both have layers of fat to keep warm.

► They are both birds, not mammals.

► They both use their flippers to swim.

Talk About It

Talk with a partner about how baby penguins are the same as and different from their parents. Write your ideas on the chart.

Same	Different

Vocabulary

Use the picture and sentence to learn each word.

adult My father is an **adult**.

What is the opposite of an adult?

alive I water the flowers to keep them **alive**.

How can you tell that a plant is alive?

covered Polar bears are **covered** with thick, white fur.

What are birds covered with?

fur My kitten has **fur** that is soft and fluffy.

What are some other animals that have fur?

giant

That **giant** tree is taller than my house.

Tell about the most giant thing you have ever seen.

groom

I use a brush to **groom** my horse each day.

What is another word for groom?

mammal

A **mammal** has fur or hair and breathes air.

Describe a mammal you know about.

offspring

At the zoo, we saw a mother rabbit and two **offspring**.

What is the name for the offspring of a dog?

Your Turn

COLLABORATE

Pick three words. Write three questions for your partner to answer.

Go Digital! **Use the online visual glossary**

Eagles and Eaglets

Inquiry Question

How do animals survive?

Bald eagles are birds. The baby birds, or **offspring** are called eaglets. Let's read about how eaglets are like their parents.

It's Nesting Time

All birds lay eggs. Bald eagles build their nests in the tops of trees so the eggs will be safe. Their nests are built of sticks and grass. They add on to their nests each year. They can become huge! These **giant** nests can be as large as nine feet across. That's bigger than your bed!

The mother eagle lays from one to three eggs. She sits on her eggs until they hatch. Then both parents watch over the nest.

Proud Parents

At first the eaglets are helpless. They cannot walk. They need their parents for food. They also cannot see well. Birds are not **mammals**. They do not have milk to feed their young. They hunt for food. Eaglets also need their parents for safety.

Eaglets Grow Up

Bald eagles use their sharp eyes to hunt. They use their strong wings to fly fast. They also use their claws and beak to catch fish. Young eaglets must learn all these things. Then they can live on their own.

The eagles must bring food to the eaglets.

Accent Alaska.com/ Alamy

Unlike mammals, birds have feathers, not **fur**. An eaglet is born **covered** with soft gray down. It cannot fly until it grows dark feathers like its parents. The eaglet stays near the nest until its wings grow strong. That takes about five months.

Bald Eagle

powerful eyes

hooked yellow beak

dark feathers on body and wings

white tail feathers

long claws

Frank Leung/Getty Images

An eaglet becomes an **adult** when it has learned to do all the things its parents do. This takes about five years. Bald eagles can stay **alive** for up to thirty years.

When the bald eagle soars, the feathers on its huge wings spread out like fingers.

Ken Canning/Getty Images

Bald Eagles Soar

Once it learns to fly, the bald eagle can soar for hours. The bald eagle must take good care of its feathers. It uses its beak to **groom** itself. It must keep its feathers clean. Can you believe this powerful eagle began life as a helpless baby?

Make Connections

How is the eaglet like its parents? How is it different?

Compare how your parents and eagle parents take care of their young. TEXT TO SELF

Reread

As you read, you may come across new words or information you don't understand. You can reread to help you understand the text.

 Find Text Evidence

On page 152 of "Eagles and Eaglets," the text tells how birds are helpless. I will go back and reread to understand how they are helpless.

page 152

Proud Parents

At first the eaglets are helpless. They cannot walk. They need their parents for food. They also cannot see well. Birds are not **mammals**. They do not have milk to feed their young. They hunt for food. Eaglets also need their parents for safety.

Eaglets Grow Up

Bald eagles use their sharp eyes to hunt. They use their strong wings to fly fast.

I read that eaglets cannot walk so they need their parents to get them food. This explains how they are helpless.

 COLLABORATE

Your Turn

Why are eagles not able to fly when they are born? Reread page 153 to help you answer the question.

Main Topic and Key Details

The main topic is what the selection is about. Key details give information about the main topic.

 Find Text Evidence

As I read page 151 I learn a lot about eagles. This must be the main topic. I also read details about eagles.

Main Topic		
Eagles		
Key Detail	**Key Detail**	**Key Detail**
Eagles build nests and lay eggs.		

Your Turn

COLLABORATE

Continue reading the story. Fill in the graphic organizer with more key details that tell about the topic.

Go Digital!
Use the interactive graphic organizer

Expository Text

The selection "Eagles and Eaglets" is an expository text. An **Expository text**:
- gives facts about a topic.
- can have text features.

Find Text Evidence

I know that "Eagles and Eaglets" is an expository text because it gives facts about eagles. It also has text features that help me learn about eagles.

page 153

Unlike mammals, birds have feathers, not **fur**. An eaglet is born **covered** with soft gray down. It cannot fly until it grows dark feathers like its parents. The eaglet stays near the nest until its wings grow strong. That takes about five months.

Bald Eagle

powerful eyes

dark feathers on body and wings

hooked yellow beak

white tail feathers

long claws

153

Text Features

A **diagram** is a picture that shows information.

The **labels** explain the parts of the diagram.

Your Turn

COLLABORATE

Tell what information you learned from looking at the diagram and reading the labels.

Multiple-Meaning Words

Multiple-meaning words have more than one meaning. Use the other words in a sentence to figure out which meaning is being used.

 Find Text Evidence

I'm not sure what the word add *means. This word could mean "to put on something extra," or it could mean "to put numbers together." Since the eagles are making a nest, I think the first meaning makes sense in this sentence.*

They add on to their nests each year.

Takayuki Maekawa/Getty Images

Your Turn

COLLABORATE

Use sentence clues to figure out the meanings of these words in "Eagles and Eaglets."
  watch, *page 151*
  fly, *page 152*

Write About the Text

Pages 150–155

Nick

I answered the question: *In your opinion, are eaglets more similar to or different from their parents? Use text evidence to support your answer.*

Student Model: *Opinion*

Topic Sentence
I state my opinion clearly in the first sentence.

Supporting Details
I included facts about the eaglets' feathers to support my opinion.

> I think eaglets are different from their parents. The text tells me that eaglets have soft gray down. Their parents have brown and white feathers. Eaglets cannot fly at first. They also cannot see clearly. Their parents must feed them and keep them safe.

160

Eaglets' parents teach them how to fly and how to hunt.

Once the eaglets grow strong, they become more like their parents. They take care of themselves. They soar through the sky just like their parents.

Grammar

Eaglets is a **plural noun**.

Grammar Handbook

See page 479.

Your Turn

In your opinion, it is easy or hard for an eagle to take care of an eaglet? Use text evidence to support your answer.

Go Digital!
Write your response online.
Use your editing checklist.

Accent Alaska.com/Alamy

Animal Fun

Animals are fun to play with. This dolphin is large, wet, and makes whistling sounds. We can use sensory words to describe animals.

► We can describe how an animal looks, feels, sounds, and smells.

► We can tell how animals behave and express themselves.

Talk About It

Use sensory words to talk with a partner about an animal you like. Write your ideas on the web.

Words That Describe a _____.

Vocabulary

Use the picture and sentence to learn each word.

behave

The boy is teaching the dog to **behave**.

How do you behave when you are in the library?

flapping

The bird was **flapping** its wings quickly.

Describe what flapping is.

express

This baby is smiling to **express** how he feels.

How do you express your feelings?

feathers

A peacock is covered in colorful **feathers**.

Where else have you seen feathers?

Poetry Words

poem

A **poem** is a form of writing that expresses imagination or feelings.

How is a poem different from a story?

rhyme

When two words **rhyme**, they have the same ending sounds.

What words could a poet use to rhyme with cat?

rhythm

Rhythm is the repeating accents, or beats, in a poem.

Why would a poet want a poem to have rhythm?

word choice

Word choice is the use of rich, colorful, exact words.

What exact word could you use to describe how you feel right now?

COLLABORATE

Your Turn

Pick three words and write a question about each for your partner to answer.

Go Digital!   *Use the online visual glossary*

Cats and Kittens

Inquiry Question

What do we love about animals?

Cats and kittens **express** their views
With hisses, purrs, and little mews.

Instead of taking baths like me,
They use their tongues quite handily.

I wonder what my mom would say
If I tried cleaning up that way.

They stay as still as still can be,
Until a mouse they chance to see.

And then in one great flash of fur
They pounce on a toy with a PURRRR.

— by Constance Keremes

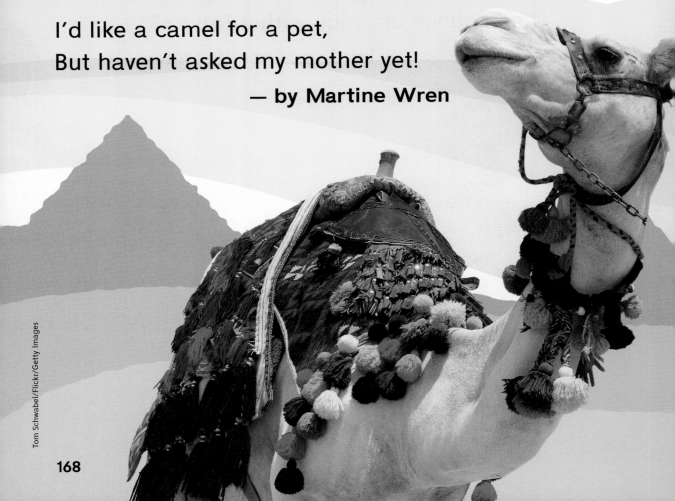

Desert Camels

Camels have a hump on their backs
To carry people and their sacks.

They're very strong, don't mind the Sun,
Won't stop for drinks until they're done.

They give people a bouncy ride.
They sway and move from side to side.

I'd like a camel for a pet,
But haven't asked my mother yet!

— **by Martine Wren**

A Bat Is Not a Bird

A bat has neither **feathers** nor beak.
He does not chirp, just gives a shriek.

He flies by hearing sounds like pings,
Flapping, flapping his leathery wings.

At night when I'm asleep in my bed,
He gets to fly around instead!

— **by Trevor Reynolds**

Make Connections

Talk about what the poet loves about the animal in each poem.

Describe how your favorite animal **behaves**. TEXT TO SELF

Rhyming Poem

A **rhyming poem**:
- has words that end with the same sounds.
- tells a poet's thoughts or feelings.

Find Text Evidence

I can tell that "Cats and Kittens" is a rhyming poem. The author tells her thoughts about cats. Also, the last words in lines one and two rhyme.

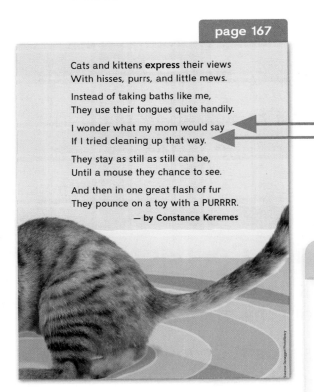

page 167

Cats and kittens **express** their views
With hisses, purrs, and little mews.

Instead of taking baths like me,
They use their tongues quite handily.

I wonder what my mom would say
If I tried cleaning up that way.

They stay as still as still can be,
Until a mouse they chance to see.

And then in one great flash of fur
They pounce on a toy with a PURRRR.

— by Constance Keremes

Sometimes pairs of lines **rhyme** in a rhyming poem.

COLLABORATE

Your Turn

Read the poems "Desert Camels" and "A Bat Is Not a Bird." Tell which lines rhyme.

Key Details

Key details give important information about a poem. You can find important information in the words, pictures, or photos.

 Find Text Evidence

As I read "Desert Camels," I understand that camels are very strong. I read that they can carry people and their sacks.

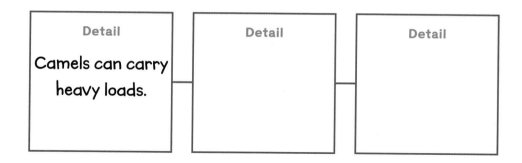

Detail		Detail		Detail
Camels can carry heavy loads.				

Your Turn

Reread "Desert Camels." Find the key details and list them in the graphic organizer.

Go Digital!
Use the interactive graphic organizer

Rhythm

Poems have rhythm. Rhythm is the repeating accents in a poem. You can clap the rhythm, or beats, in a poem.

 Find Text Evidence

Reread "Desert Camels," and listen to the rhythm. Listen to the beats in each line. Think about why the poet uses rhythm.

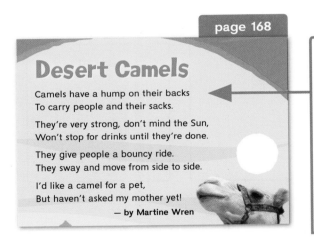

page 168

Desert Camels

Camels have a hump on their backs
To carry people and their sacks.

They're very strong, don't mind the Sun,
Won't stop for drinks until they're done.

They give people a bouncy ride.
They sway and move from side to side.

I'd like a camel for a pet,
But haven't asked my mother yet!

— by Martine Wren

I clap the beats in the first line. There are eight beats. There are also eight beats in the second line. The beats make the poem fun to read.

Your Turn

COLLABORATE

Clap the first two lines of "Cats and Kittens." Tell if the rhythm is the same as "Desert Camels" or different.

Multiple-Meaning Words

Multiple-meaning words are words that are spelled the same but have more than one meaning. You can use context clues to help you understand the correct meaning.

 Find Text Evidence

In "A Bat Is Not a Bird," I see the word bat. *I know a bat is an animal and also something you use to play baseball. The words "feathers" and "beak" tell me the author is talking about an animal.*

page 169

A **bat** has neither feathers nor beak.

COLLABORATE

Your Turn

Reread the poems "A Bat Is Not a Bird" and "Desert Camels." Use context clues to decide on the meaning of these words:
   flies, "A Bat Is Not a Bird"
   pet, "Desert Camels"

Photri Images/Alamy

Pages 166–169

Write About the Text

Martin

I responded to the prompt: *Pick an animal and write a rhyming poem. Think about how the use of rhyme focuses your thoughts and feelings.*

Precise Words
I chose specific words and details to make my meaning clear.

Grammar

The word *chick's* is an example of a **possessive noun**.

Grammar Handbook

See page 480.

Student Model: *Narrative Text*

Baby Chicks

Baby chicks are small and sweet.

Holding them is such a treat!

Chick's feathers are oh so fluffy.

They're so nice, never huffy.

Details
I told how it feels to hold baby chicks.

Chicks become roosters or hens,

living in little houses called pens.

Little chicks are baby birds.

Chirpy cheeps, instead of words.

Rhyme

I used rhyming words to add form to my poem about baby chicks.

Your Turn

Write your own rhyming poem about an animal. Think about how the use of rhyme focuses your thoughts and feelings about the animal.

Go Digital!
Write your response online.
Use your editing checklist.

Contents

Sentences

Sentences

A **sentence** tells a complete thought.

Tom feeds the cat.

Your Turn Write each group of words. Write "complete" next to the complete sentence.

1. The dog runs outside.
2. Digs in the yard.

Kinds of Sentences

Every sentence begins with a **capital letter** and ends with an **end mark**.

A **statement** tells something. It ends with a period.	*Tara can read music.*
A **question** asks something. It ends with a question mark.	*Do you like this song?*
A **command** tells someone to do something. It ends with a period.	*Sing along with me.*
An **exclamation** shows strong feeling. It ends with an exclamation mark.	*We sound great together!*

Your Turn Write each sentence. Then tell what kind of sentence it is.

1. Anna plays in a band.
2. Does she sing?
3. We love the new song!
4. Listen to the drums.

Subjects in Sentences

The **subject** in a sentence tells who or what does something.

Our teacher reads the story.

Your Turn Write each sentence. Underline the subject.

1. Ann listens to the news.
2. Mom looks outside.
3. Strong winds begin to blow.
4. Ann and Mom make plans.
5. The family prepares for the storm.

Predicates in Sentences

The **predicate** in a sentence tells what the subject does or is.

Our teacher reads the story.

Your Turn Write each sentence. Underline each predicate.

1. Rosa listens to the news.
2. She hears about the storm.
3. Her two brothers close the windows.
4. Everyone is excited.
5. The heavy rain falls at night.

Sentences

Combining Sentences: Subjects

When two sentences have the same predicate, you can use the word **and** to combine the subjects.

Trina <u>went to the movies</u>. Kim <u>went to the movies</u>.
Trina <u>and</u> Kim went to the movies.

Your Turn Use *and* to combine each pair of sentences. Write the new sentence.

1. Shawn sat down. Kent sat down.
2. Brianna wanted pizza. Kent wanted pizza.
3. The pizza smelled good. The pasta smelled good.
4. Kent asked for water. I asked for water.
5. Brianna thanked the waiter. Shawn thanked the waiter.

Nouns

A **noun** is a word that names a person, place, or thing.

My brother left his book at the library.

   ↑   ↑   ↑

person   thing   place

Your Turn Write each sentence. Draw a line under each noun.

1. My family lives in a small town.
2. Our father works in the city.
3. The cousins share stories.

Common and Proper Nouns

Common nouns name general people, places, or things.

The <u>woman</u> drives her <u>car</u> down the <u>street</u>.

Proper nouns name specific people, places, or things.

<u>Jenny</u> walks <u>Whiskers</u> down <u>Park Street</u>.

Your Turn Write each sentence. Underline each common noun. Circle each proper noun.

1. My cousins are going to Mexico.
2. Their plane leaves from Chicago.
3. Lori will bring a camera.
4. My family will stay on Pine Street.

Nouns

Days, Months, and Holidays

Some proper nouns name **days of the week, months,** and **holidays.** They begin with capital letters.

> *Our homework is due on <u>Monday</u>. (day of the week)*
> *My birthday is in <u>April</u>. (month of the year)*
> *We will travel for <u>Thanksgiving</u>. (holiday)*

Your Turn Write each sentence correctly. Begin each proper noun with a capital letter.

1. School is closed next monday.
2. It will be memorial day.
3. This was the warmest may ever.

Singular and Plural Nouns

A noun that names only one thing is **singular**.

A noun that names more than one thing is **plural**.

Add *-s* to form the plural of most nouns.

> *The large river split into two <u>rivers</u>.*

Add *-es* to form the plural of nouns that end in *s, sh, ch,* or *x. This box is bigger than the other <u>boxes</u>.*

Your Turn Write each sentence. Make the noun in ( ) name more than one.

1. I have two (wish).
2. First, I need new (sock).
3. Next, I want three (book).

More Plural Nouns

If a word ends in a consonant plus *y*, change the *y* to *i* and add *-es* to form the plural.

My mother's <u>berry</u> pie has three kinds of <u>berries</u>.

Some nouns change their spelling to name more than one. Others don't change at all.

Singular	Plural
man	men
woman	women
child	children
tooth	teeth
mouse	mice
foot	feet
fish	fish
sheep	sheep

Your Turn **Write each sentence. Make the noun in ( ) name more than one.**

1. The (child) went to a farm.
2. How many (sheep) did they see?
3. The barn was thirty (foot) high!
4. Four (pony) played in a field.
5. Workers picked (cherry) from the trees.

Nouns

Collective Nouns

A **collective noun** names a group that acts together as a singular thing.

The _team_ runs out onto the field.

Your Turn Write each sentence. Underline each collective noun.

1. My family plays music.
2. I may start a band.
3. The group needs to practice.

Singular and Plural Possessive Nouns

A **possessive noun** is a noun that shows who or what owns something. Add an **apostrophe (')** and an *-s* to a singular noun to make it possessive.

The dog grabbed our _father's_ hat.

Add just an apostrophe to most plural nouns to make them possessive. *The two _brothers'_ bikes are both red.*

Add an apostrophe and an *-s* to form the possessive of plural nouns that do not end in *-s*.

The men went to get the _women's_ coats.

Your Turn Write each sentence. Use the possessive form of the noun in ( ) .

1. I study at my (friend) house.
2. What are his (parents) names?
3. Listen to the (children) songs!

Action Verbs

An **action verb** is a word that shows action.

The runners <u>race</u> to the finish line.

Your Turn Write each sentence. Draw a line under each action verb.

1. We drive to the beach.
2. My father swims in the ocean.
3. My sisters build a sand castle.
4. My brother collects shells and rocks.
5. Mom dives into the water and splashes us.

Linking Verbs

A **linking verb** connects the subject to the rest of the sentence. It does not show action. Linking verbs include: *be, am, is, are, was, were, will be.*

Our teacher <u>is</u> a wonderful actor.

Your Turn Write each sentence. Draw a line under each linking verb.

1. The class play is a comedy.
2. The lines are hard to learn.
3. My best friends were clowns.
4. I am excited about my role.
5. The setting will be a circus.

Verbs

Present-Tense Verbs

Present-tense verbs tell what is happening now.
Add *-s* or *-es* to tell what one person or thing is doing.

The man <u>looks</u> at the sky. He <u>watches</u> the dark clouds.

Your Turn Write each sentence in the present tense. Use the correct form of the verb in ( ).

1. The rain (start) to fall.
2. The horse (run) into the barn.
3. Water (rush) down the hill.

Past-Tense Verbs

Past-tense verbs tell about actions in the past. Most past-tense verbs end with *-ed*.

The players <u>kicked</u> the ball into the woods.

For verbs like *drop*, double the final consonant before adding *-ed*.
For verbs like *race*, drop the *e* before adding *-ed*.

The principal <u>tapped</u> the glass and <u>raised</u> the window.

Your Turn Write each sentence in the past tense. Use the correct form of the verb in ( ).

1. The coach (shout) at us.
2. We (stop) what we were doing.
3. The coach (dare) us to run another mile.

Future-Tense Verbs

Future-tense verbs tell about action that is going to happen. Use the verb *will* to write about the future.

Next year, my family <u>will visit</u> our relatives.

Your Turn Write each sentence in the future tense. Use the correct form of each verb in ( ).

1. We (drive) over five hundred miles.
2. My grandparents (be) happy to see us.
3. I (write) letters to all my friends.
4. We (call) each other when we can.
5. I (start) a journal and (take) many pictures.

Subject-Verb Agreement

A **subject** and **verb** must agree. Add *-s* or *-es* only if the subject tells about one person or thing in the present tense.

My <u>mother calls</u> us, and <u>we come</u> right away.

Your Turn Write each sentence. Use the correct form of each verb in ( ).

1. The hikers (climb) the mountain.
2. The guide (choose) a spot for the tent.
3. The group (rest) for a while.
4. The cook (start) a fire and (make) dinner.
5. Last year, they (camp) here as well.

Verbs

The Verb *Have*

Use **have** with most subjects in the present tense.
For one person or thing, use **has**.

Use **had** for the past tense.

> I *have* a red shirt. The girl *has* a blue shirt. We both *had* black shoes.

Your Turn Write each sentence. Use the correct form of the verb *have*.

1. My mother (have) a question.
2. I (have) the answer.
3. Last fall, my sisters (have) a contest.

The Verb *Be*

For the present tense, use **is** if the subject is singular.
Use **am** if the subject is *I*. Use **are** if the subject is plural or *you*.

For the past tense, use **was** if the subject is singular or *I*. Use **were** if the subject is plural or *you*.

> Ann *is* the leader this year, but I *was* leader last year.

Your Turn Write each sentence. Use the correct form of the verb *be*.

1. I (is) at the library.
2. You (is) at school.
3. Yesterday, Dad (is) at home.
4. Last week, we (is) all on vacation.

Contractions with *Not*

A **contraction** is a short form of two words. An **apostrophe** shows where one or more letters have been left out. Two irregular contractions are **can't** (can not) and **won't** (will not).

This <u>isn't</u> easy. You <u>aren't</u> ready. They <u>don't</u> want to go.

Your Turn Write each sentence. Form a contraction using the words in ( ).

1. My friend (did not) read the book.
2. The questions (are not) difficult.
3. Our teacher (does not) give us much time.
4. We (will not) finish before lunch.

Helping Verbs

A **helping verb** helps another verb show action. *Am, is* and *are* can help tell about action in the present. *Has* and *had* can help tell about action in the past.

Jess <u>is</u> telling a story. We <u>had</u> heard it before.

Your Turn Write each sentence. Underline the helping verb.

1. The boy is building a fort.
2. His father has helped him in the past.
3. We are watching them raise the roof.
4. Now I am bringing them lunch.

Verbs

Irregular Verbs

An **irregular verb** has a special spelling to show the past tense. Some also have a special spelling when used with the helping verb *have*.

Present	Past
come	came
do	did
eat	ate
give	gave
go	went
hide	hid
run	ran
say	said
see	saw
sing	sang
sit	sat
take	took
tell	told
write	wrote

Your Turn Write each sentence in the past tense. Use the correct form of the verb in ( ).

1. My friends (come) to my house yesterday.
2. Last weekend they (run) a race.
3. I (see) them training.
4. My friends (say) they would win.
5. They (go) fast and (do) well.

Combining Sentences: Verbs

When two sentences have the same subject, you can use the word **and** to combine the predicates.

<u>Taylor</u> *swings the bat.* <u>Taylor</u> *hits the ball.*

Taylor swings the bat <u>and</u> hits the ball.

Your Turn Use *and* **to combine each pair of sentences. Write the new sentence.**

1. My dad sings. My dad dances.
2. Paul claps. Paul stomps his feet.
3. Mother plays piano. Mother hums.
4. Jean is tired. Jean sits down.
5. We are having fun. We don't want to stop.

Pronouns

Pronouns: *I, You, He, She, It, We, They*

A **pronoun** takes the place of one or more nouns. The pronouns *I, you, he, she, it, we,* and *they* can be used as subjects in a sentence.

I like to ski. You and he like to surf.

Your Turn Write each sentence. Replace the underline word or words with a pronoun.

1. My friend lives near the beach.
2. The house is very small.
3. Mom has a sailboat.
4. My friend and I like to swim.
5. Are his brother and sister good swimmers, too?

Pronouns: *Me, You, Him, Her, It, Us, Them*

Some **pronouns** come after the verb in a sentence. The pronouns *me, you, him, her, it, us,* and *them* can be used in the predicate of a sentence.

Dad gave him the pen. He used it to write a poem.

Your Turn Write each sentence. Replace the underlined word or words with a pronoun.

1. We held the fair outside.
2. The rain soaked the boys and girls.
3. Who gave my sister an umbrella?
4. I saw my father inside his car.
5. An oak tree kept my friend and me dry.

Pronouns with *-self* and *-selves*

Some pronouns in the predicate tell about an action that a subject does for or to itself. The ending **-self** is used for singular pronouns. The ending **-selves** is used for plural pronouns.

The boy made <u>himself</u> a snack. We gave <u>ourselves</u> a pear.

Your Turn **Write each sentence. Replace the word or words in ( ) with a pronoun.**

1. My brother teaches (my brother) Spanish.
2. My mother asks (my mother) a question.
3. Could my parents teach (my parents) French?
4. The computer shuts (the computer) off.

Possessive Pronouns

A **possessive pronoun** takes the place of a possessive noun. It shows who or what owns something. *My, your, her, his, its, our,* and *their* are possessive pronouns.

I gave <u>my</u> homework to <u>our</u> teacher.

Your Turn **Write each sentence. Replace the underlined words with a possessive pronoun.**

1. <u>My sister's</u> room faces east.
2. She can see <u>the school's</u> playground.
3. <u>The building's</u> walls are made of brick.
4. <u>The teacher's</u> cars are parked nearby.
5. <u>My sister's and my</u> walk to school is short.

Pronouns

Pronoun-Verb Agreement

The verb of a sentence must agree with the pronoun that is the subject of the verb.

> *She laughs* while *we perform* our play.

Your Turn **Write each sentence. Use the correct present-tense form of the verb in ( ).**

1. She (draw) a map.
2. It (show) how to get to the lake.
3. We (hope) to get there by noon.
4. They (think) we may be lost.
5. Where (do) she think she is going?

Contractions

A **contraction** can be the short form of a pronoun combined with a verb. An **apostrophe** takes the place of the letters that are left out.

I'm sorry that you'll miss class today.

Your Turn **Write each sentence. Replace the underlined contraction with a pronoun and a verb.**

1. He's worried about the sick dog.
2. We're about to call the doctor.
3. Do you think she'll be able to help?
4. We hope it's not serious.
5. You'll soon feel better than ever!

Adjectives

Adjectives

An **adjective** is a word that describes a noun. Some adjectives tell what **kind** or how **many**.

Three dogs with <u>red</u> collars ran down the <u>dark</u> street.

Your Turn Write each sentence. Circle each adjective and underline the noun being described.

1. We'll need four apples for the pie.
2. Bake it for sixty minutes.
3. I prefer a thin crust.
4. Don't touch the hot plate!
5. Could I become a famous chef?

Articles

The words *the, a,* and *an* are special adjectives called **articles**. Use *a* before words that begin with consonant sounds. Use *an* before words that begin with vowel sounds.

<u>An</u> owl built <u>the</u> nest high in <u>a</u> tree.

Your Turn Write each sentence. Circle the articles.

1. A fox ran through our yard.
2. It woke up the dog.
3. I turned on a light outside.
4. A pair of eyes glowed in the dark.
5. I shut off the light in an instant.

This, That, These, and *Those*

This, that, these, and *those* are special adjectives that tell how many and how close. **This** and **that** refer to singular nouns. **These** and **those** refer to plural nouns.

> *I will read <u>these</u> books in my arms before I read <u>those</u> books on the shelf.*

Your Turn **Write each sentence. Choose the correct adjective in ( ) to complete the sentence.**

1. My sister enjoys (this, these) movie.
2. I like (that, those) actors.
3. (This, These) special effects are great.
4. (That, Those) monster scared me.
5. I would watch (these, this) movie again.

Adjectives That Compare

Add *-er* to an adjective to compare two nouns. Add *-est* to compare more than two nouns.

> *Bill is <u>taller</u> than me, but Steve is my <u>tallest</u> brother.*

Your Turn **Write each sentence. Add *-er* or *-est* to the adjective in ( ).**

1. My mom wants a (fast) car than our old one.
2. She looks at the (new) model of all the cars.
3. Does this car have a (high) price than that one?
4. This was the (hard) decision we've ever made!
5. Is one car is (safe) than another?

493

Adverbs and Prepositional Phrases

Adverbs

An **adverb** is a word that tells more about a verb. Adverbs tell *how, when,* or *where*. Many adverbs end in *-ly. We ran* <u>quickly</u> *to the front of the line.*

Your Turn **Write each sentence. Circle each adverb. Then underline the verb it tells about.**

1. I listened closely to the news.
2. The storm moved slowly out to sea.
3. We walked outside to check the sky.

Prepositional Phrases

A **preposition** comes before a noun or a pronoun. Together they make a **prepositional phrase**. Common prepositions include *in, at, of, from, with, to,* and *by*. A prepositional phrase can work as an adjective or an adverb that tells *how, when,* or *where*.

We ran quickly <u>to the front</u> <u>of the line</u>.

Your Turn **Write each sentence. Underline the prepositional phrase. Circle the preposition.**

1. I walked to the park.
2. Did you go with your friends?
3. We helped put trash in bags.
4. We did something good for our community.

Abbreviations

An **abbreviation** is a short form of a word. It usually ends with a period.

Main Street	*Main <u>St.</u>*
Lincoln Road	*Lincoln <u>Rd.</u>*
North Avenue	*North <u>Ave.</u>*
Apartment 6B	*<u>Apt.</u> 6B*
Mount Olympus	*<u>Mt.</u> Olympus*

Your Turn **Write each address using an abbreviation.**

1. 32 Front Street
2. 291 Jefferson Avenue
3. 7 Old Mill Road
4. Apartment 8H
5. 96 Mount Shasta Avenue

Titles

The abbreviation of a **title** before a name begins with a capital letter and ends with a period. Common titles before names are *Mr., Ms., Mrs.,* and *Dr.*

<u>Ms.</u> Choi invited <u>Dr.</u> Shaw and <u>Mr.</u> Howe to the show.

Your Turn **Write each name and abbreviation correctly.**

1. ms. Ellen Daly
2. Mr Mark Bryant
3. dr denise Putnam
4. mrs. june lee

Mechanics: Abbreviations

Days of the Week/Months of the Year

When you abbreviate the days of the week or the months of the year, begin with a capital letter and end with a period. Do not abbreviate *May, June,* or *July*.

Sun.   Mon.   Tues.   Wed.   Thurs.   Fri.   Sat.

Jan. Feb. Mar. Apr. Aug. Sept. Oct. Nov. Dec.

Your Turn **Write each sentence with the correct abbreviation.**

1. Our first meeting was on January 23, 2005.
2. The report is due on November 5.
3. Can you come to a party on April 17?
4. No one likes to meet on Saturday or Sunday.
5. We will meet again on Thursday, March 12.

States

When you write an address, you may use United States Postal Service abbreviations for the names of states. The abbreviations are two capital letters with no period at the end.

Alabama	AL	Kentucky	KY	Ohio	OH
Alaska	AK	Louisiana	LA	Oklahoma	OK
Arizona	AZ	Maine	ME	Oregon	OR
Arkansas	AR	Maryland	MD	Pennsylvania	PA
California	CA	Massachusetts	MA	Rhode Island	RI
Colorado	CO	Michigan	MI	South Carolina	SC
Connecticut	CT	Minnesota	MN	South Dakota	SD
Delaware	DE	Mississippi	MS	Tennessee	TN
District of		Missouri	MO	Texas	TX
Columbia	DC	Montana	MT	Utah	UT
Florida	FL	Nebraska	NE	Vermont	VT
Georgia	GA	Nevada	NV	Virginia	VA
Hawaii	HI	New Hampshire	NH	Washington	WA
Idaho	ID	New Jersey	NJ	West Virginia	WV
Illinois	IL	New Mexico	NM	Wisconsin	WI
Indiana	IN	New York	NY	Wyoming	WY
Iowa	IA	North Carolina	NC		
Kansas	KS	North Dakota	ND		

Your Turn Write the U.S. Postal Service Abbreviation for each of the following.

1. Chicago, Illinois
2. Dallas, Texas
3. Miami, Florida
4. Los Angeles, California

Mechanics: Capitalization

First Word in a Sentence

The first word in a sentence begins with a capital letter. A **quotation** is the exact words of a person speaking. The first word in a quotation begins with a capital letter.

_O_ur teacher said, "_R_emember to pack up your books."

Your Turn Write each sentence. Use capital letters correctly.

1. our coach talked to the team.
2. he said, "keep your eyes on the ball."
3. I asked, "can we practice our kicking?"

Letters

All of the words in a letter's greeting begin with a capital letter. Only the first word in the closing of a letter begins with a capital letter. Use a comma after the greeting and closing of a friendly letter.

Dear Sir,   _Yours truly,_

Your Turn Write each part of a letter with the correct capitalization.

1. dear mr. holland,
2. sincerely yours,
3. dear dr. andrews,
4. best wishes,

Names and Titles of People

The names of people begin with a capital letter. Titles begin with a capital letter. Always write the pronoun *I* as a capital letter.

Mrs. Walker and I built a bird feeder.

Your Turn **Write each sentence. Use capital letters correctly.**

1. Mr. taylor agreed to be our tour guide.
2. i think mrs. Shea is a better choice.
3. She knows dr. Peter miller.

Names of Places and Geographic Names

The names of streets, buildings, cities, and states begin with a capital letter. The names of rivers, mountains, countries, continents, and planets begin with a capital letter.

You can view Mars at Mount Evans Observatory in Colorado.

Your Turn **Write each sentence. Use capital letters correctly.**

1. We drive to washington to see the columbia river.
2. The river runs between portland and vancouver.
3. We may also visit mount st. helens.

Mechanics: Capitalization

More Proper Nouns and Adjectives

The names of schools, clubs, teams, and businesses begin with a capital letter. The names of products begin with a capital letter.

The Elmwood School Ramblers sell their Healthy Serving snacks at the bake sale.

The days of the week, months of the year, and holidays begin with a capital letter. The names of the seasons do not begin with a capital letter.

Labor Day is the first Monday in September.

Most abbreviations begin with a capital letter.

Mr. Ellis spoke with Dr. Garcia about his illness.

The first, last, and most important words in the title of a book, poem, song, story, play, movie, magazine, or newspaper begin with capital letters.

My father reads the <u>New York Times</u> while I watch <u>Alice in Wonderland</u>.

Your Turn Write each sentence. Use capital letters correctly.

1. This year february begins on a friday.
2. How will ms. davis celebrate valentine's day?
3. The mill river band is performing today.
4. The concert began with "america the beautiful."

End Marks

A **statement** is a sentence that tells a complete thought. It ends with a **period (.)**.

A **question** is a sentence that asks something. It ends with a **question mark (?)**.

A **command** is a sentence that tells someone to do something. It ends with a **period (.)**.

An **exclamation** is a sentence that shows strong feeling. It ends with an **exclamation mark (!)**.

Do you like black beans? They are my absolute favorite! I like them with rice.

Your Turn Write each sentence. Add the correct end mark.

1. We can make soup for lunch
2. Do we have enough vegetables
3. This soup will be the best ever

Periods

Use a period to show the end of an abbreviation. Use a period with initials that stand for a person's name.

On Oct. 23, Bill loaned me a book by C. S. Lewis.

Your Turn Write each sentence. Use periods correctly.

1. Mr Greco and his son joined us.
2. My mother read a book by j d salinger.
3. Oct and Nov are the best months to visit.

Mechanics: Punctuation

Commas

Use a **comma (,)** between the names of cities and states.

Austin, Texas   *Albany, New York*   *Boston, Mass.*

Use a **comma** between the day and the year in dates.

June 5, 1977   *Sept. 18, 2010*

Use a **comma** after the greeting and closing in a friendly letter.

Dear Grandma,   *Best wishes,*

Use **commas** to separate words in a series.

She took pictures of the alligators, otters, and parrots.

Use a **comma** after the words *yes* or *no* or the name of a person being spoken to.

Yes, I know Ben. Tracy, have you met him?

Use a **comma** after a sequence word.

First, we walk. Next, we take the bus.

Your Turn **Write each sentence. Add commas where needed.**

1. Dear Aunt Polly
2. I hope you like living in Portland Maine.
3. Were you born on July 4 1976?
4. Do you like parades picnics and fireworks?

Apostrophes

Use an **apostrophe (')** with a noun to show possession. Use an apostrophe in a contraction to show where a letter or letters are missing.

My brother's cat won't come in from the rain.

Your Turn Write each sentence. Add apostrophes where needed.

1. Our familys pets had a bad day.
2. The cats tail got stuck in the door.
3. Our dogs cant find their toys.
4. The door on the birds cage wont open.
5. Youll have to bring it to Mr. Swansons shop.

Quotation Marks

Use quotation marks at the beginning and at the end of the exact words a person says.

My uncle asked, "Where is your bike?"

"I left it at the shop," I replied.

Your Turn Write each sentence. Add quotation marks where needed.

1. My sister said, Your tire is flat.
2. I ran over some rocks, I replied.
3. She asked, What will you do now?
4. I need to get home right now! I exclaimed.
5. Can I borrow yours? I asked.

Mechanics: Punctuation

Italics or Underlining

Use italics or an underline for the title of a book, movie, magazine, or newspaper.

<u>James and the Giant Peach</u>   *Dolphin Tale*

Your Turn **Write each sentence. Use italics or underline the titles.**

1. I read the book My Side of the Mountain.
2. The magazine Film Fun said it was also a movie.
3. "Was it as good as The Incredible Journey?" you asked.
4. The Santa Monica Herald didn't think so.
5. Let's watch Finding Nemo again tonight.